by J. G. Minyard

Minneapolis, Minnesota

Credits
Cover, © Xinhua News Agency / Contributor/Getty Images; 4, © welcomia/iStock; 4–5, © lovelyday12/iStock; 6, © DavorLovincic/iStock; 7, © PhotoAlto sas/Alamy Stock Photo; 8, © EmirMemedovski/iStock; 9, © DuxX/iStock; 10, © Velvetfish/iStock; 11, © SolStock/iStock; 12, © fotosav/iStock; 12–13, © Tyler Stableford/Getty Images; 14, © fotog/Getty Images; 15, © bluecinema/Getty Images; 16, © Tech. Sgt. Michael Holzworth/DVIDS; 17, © HIGH-G Productions/Stocktrek Images/Getty Images; 18, © PeopleImages/iStock; 18–19, © Pramote Polyamate/Alamy Stock Photo; 20, © Yuri Arcurs/Alamy Stock Photo; 21, © Photo 12/Alamy Stock Photo; 22, © Design Pics Inc/Alamy Stock Photo; 22–23, © Ivan Bruno/iStock; 24, © SimonSkafar/Getty Images; 25, © Andrii Yalanskyi/iStock; 26, © kali9/Getty Images; 27, © Prostock-Studio/iStock; 28TL, © kali9/iStock; 28TR, © bluecinema/Getty Images; 28BL, © AzmanJaka/Getty Images; 28BR, © Kgrif/iStock; 29, © The Laura Flanders Show/Wikimedia Commons; 31, © DonNichols/iStock; 32, © malerapaso/iStock.

Bearport Publishing Company Product Development Team
Publisher: Jen Jenson; Director of Product Development: Spencer Brinker; Managing Editor: Allison Juda; Editor: Cole Nelson; Associate Editor: Naomi Reich; Associate Editor: Tiana Tran; Art Director: Colin O'Dea; Designer: Kim Jones; Designer: Kayla Eggert; Product Development Specialist: Owen Hamlin

Statement on Usage of Generative Artificial Intelligence
Bearport Publishing remains committed to publishing high-quality nonfiction books. Therefore, we restrict the use of generative AI to ensure accuracy of all text and visual components pertaining to a book's subject. See BearportPublishing.com for details.

Library of Congress Cataloging-in-Publication Data is available at www.loc.gov or upon request from the publisher.

ISBN: 979-8-89232-646-9 (hardcover)
ISBN: 979-8-89232-679-7 (ebook)

For more information, write to Bearport Publishing, 5357 Penn Avenue South, Minneapolis, MN 55419.

CONTENTS

HEAD-TO-HEAD WITH DANGER

Many people would run at the sight of fiery explosions and zapping wires. But for some, it's just another day at work. These brave workers face many dangers to provide us with services that make our lives easier, safer, and more exciting. Whether it's testing aircraft or rescuing people from burning buildings, these professionals rise to the challenge to get the job done. Let's explore dangerous jobs on the edge!

People may think jobs like farming and garbage collecting are safe and easy. But these everyday jobs can be some of the most dangerous ones!

LOOK OUT BELOW!

Logger

Working in the lumber industry is not easy. Loggers use chain saws to cut down tall trees. Sometimes, they don't even know where the trees will fall until moments before they come crashing down! But that's not the only thing loggers have to look out for. They must also be careful to avoid breathing in **sawdust** and to keep their fingers intact while working with sharp equipment.

What It Takes

- ☑ Strength to lift heavy objects
- ☑ An ability to work in all types of weather
- ☑ Knowledge of different types of wood
- ☑ Extra caution
- ☑ A loud and booming voice

After loggers cut down trees, they often drag the lumber to a loading site or staging area.

Loggers often use handheld chain saws to cut trees.

Loggers provide people with trees to make paper and other wood products.

LONG HAUL

Truck Driver

Unlike most people, truck drivers often work as many as 70 hours a week to deliver goods from one place to another. These workers are constantly on the road, having little time to sleep. But falling asleep behind the wheel could lead to a deadly crash. Even with fully awake drivers, trucks can be dangerous. Since they are such large vehicles, trucks have bigger **blind spots** than most cars. It also takes them longer to slow down.

What It Takes

- ☑ A commercial driver's license
- ☑ A passion for traveling
- ☑ Lots and lots of coffee
- ☑ A love of spending time alone

These drivers need to make sure deliveries are on time.

On average, a truck driver travels more than 100,000 miles (160,000 km) every year.

There are tens of thousands of driving accidents with trucks every year.

DANGEROUS CATCH

Lobster Fisher

Catching lobsters isn't as simple as tossing a net. Things can turn deadly if the job isn't done carefully! Fishing workers use traps connected to a **buoy** to catch lobsters. Later, these fishers pull their traps back up to see what they've caught. That's when things get dangerous. Sometimes, lobster fishers become entangled in their own traps and are pulled overboard. Once in the icy waters, the workers could easily drown.

What It Takes

- ☑ Strong arms for hauling traps
- ☑ A good pair of sea legs
- ☑ A federal lobster permit
- ☑ Being unafraid of snapping claws

The doors on lobster traps are funnel shaped, making them easy to walk into but hard to get out of.

Lobster fishers wait a few hours before pulling their traps back up to see what they've caught.

Fishers usually need to catch about 150 pounds (70 kg) of lobsters to pay for the bait and gas used for fishing.

SOUND THE ALARM

Firefighter

Firefighters are the first to run into fiery danger. While helping those in need, these heroes face the risks of falling buildings and breathing in toxic chemicals. But firefighters do more than just put out fires. They also save people trapped in cars, handle **hazardous** materials, and help with medical emergencies.

What It Takes

- ☑ Physical fitness
- ☑ Medical knowledge
- ☑ Good judgment
- ☑ A lot of bravery
- ☑ A passion for helping others
- ☑ Strength to carry people to safety

Fire hydrants allow firefighters to access the water they need.

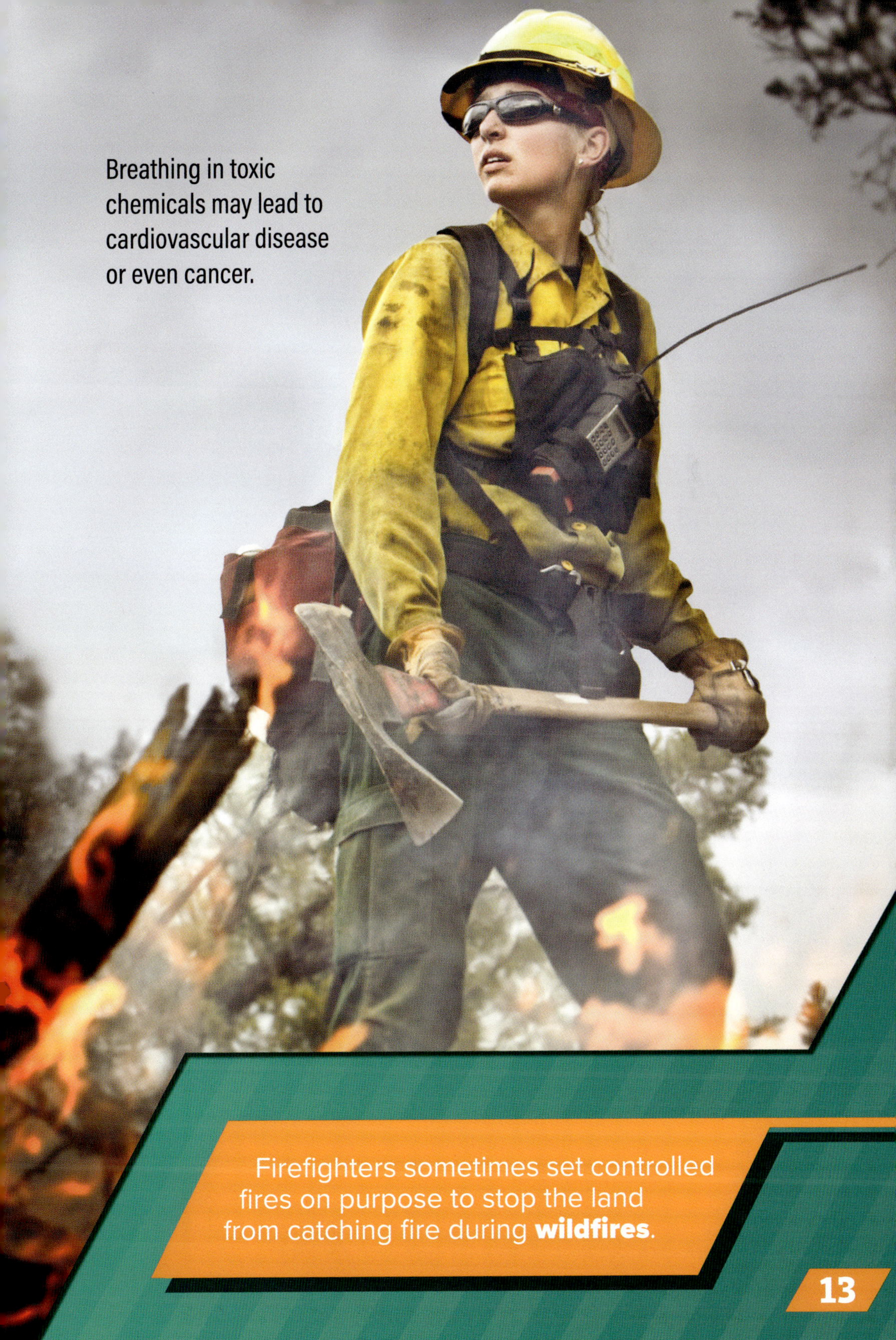

Breathing in toxic chemicals may lead to cardiovascular disease or even cancer.

Firefighters sometimes set controlled fires on purpose to stop the land from catching fire during **wildfires**.

WATCH YOUR STEP!

High-Rise Window Washer

High-rise window washers keep skyscraper windows squeaky-clean. These fearless cleaners are **suspended** hundreds of feet in the air, with only cables stopping them from falling to their doom. They often have to work in windy conditions, heavy **precipitation**, and sweltering heat. Sometimes, they even have to dodge the sharp beaks and claws of swooping birds. The window washers are on constant alert since just one slip could spell disaster!

What It Takes

- ☑ Being unafraid of heights
- ☑ Attention to detail
- ☑ Physical stamina
- ☑ Cleaning experience
- ☑ Patience

These cleaners often work on wide, suspended platforms for efficiency and safety.

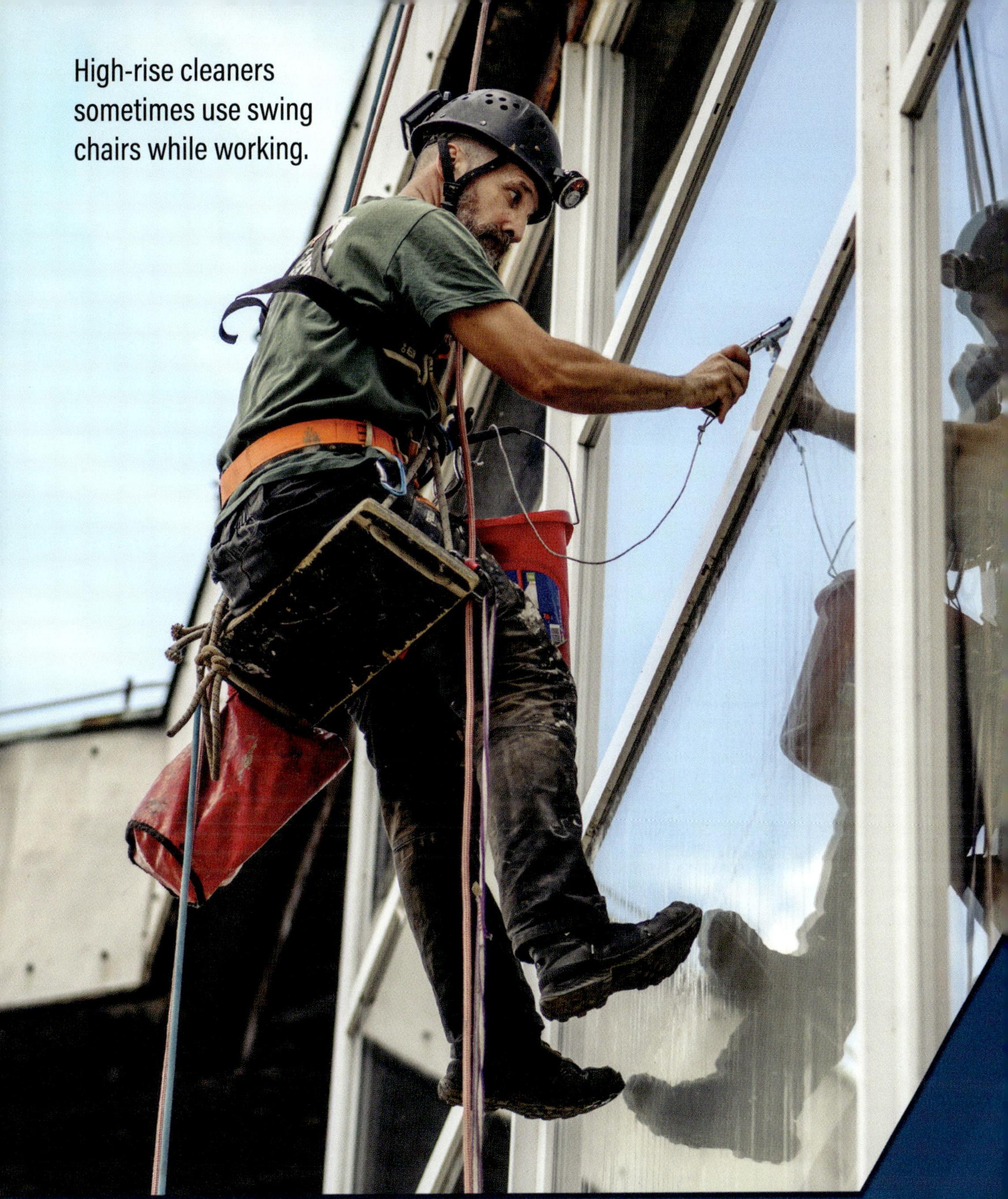

High-rise cleaners sometimes use swing chairs while working.

Engineers are working on designing and building robots to help with window washing.

READY FOR TAKEOFF

Test Pilot

Before aircraft are cleared for flight, they need to be checked for safety. That's where test pilots come in. Their job is to make sure newly built aircraft work the way they're supposed to. These pilots run performance tests in many different conditions, such as in extreme cold or high speed. Since they're testing machines that have never been used, the pilots need to be prepared for anything—even parts failing mid-flight!

What It Takes

- ☑ A pilot's license
- ☑ Being calm under pressure
- ☑ A daredevil attitude
- ☑ Flying experience
- ☑ An engineering degree
- ☑ Steady hands

Test pilots wear oxygen masks to help them breathe while flying the aircraft.

The cockpit of an aircraft contains communication and navigation controls.

From **commercial planes** to military jets, all kinds of aircraft need test pilots to make sure they are safe.

DOWN AND DIRTY

Garbage Collector

The task of garbage collectors is all in the name—they pick up and transport trash. They drive around communities, making one stop after another. Sometimes, these frequent stops can cause accidents with passing vehicles. Garbage collectors use special trucks to gather the waste, but if trash falls out, they need to pick it up by hand. This means garbage collectors must watch out for broken glass, stray needles, and dangerous chemicals.

What It Takes

- ☑ Maintaining a clean work environment
- ☑ An ability to lift heavy things
- ☑ Standing for long hours
- ☑ A strong stomach

Some collectors ride on the back of trucks as they go from stop to stop.

Garbage collectors often need to lift heavy containers.

Sometimes, garbage collectors must help law **enforcement** search through trash for **evidence**.

LIGHTS, CAMERA, EXPLOSION!

Stunt Performer

From acrobatics to **parkour**, stunt performers do it all. These trained professionals perform the daring and dangerous moves for movies, TV shows, and other productions. They sometimes perform action scenes in freezing waters or sweltering heat. But that's only just the beginning of the dangerous work these daredevils do. Stunt performers may fall from tall buildings, jump in front of **rigged** explosives, or even take a punch or two from the story's hero.

What It Takes

- ☑ Physical fitness
- ☑ An ability to take a hit
- ☑ Being calm under pressure
- ☑ A daredevil attitude

Stage combat classes help stunt performers make action scenes look realistic.

Some stunt performers are trained in martial arts. This prepares them for fight scenes.

During rehearsals, stunt performers practice over and over again until the moves are perfect.

HIGH VOLTAGE

Line Worker

Line workers are essential to keeping power flowing to homes and businesses. They **scale** wooden **power line** poles to install and maintain electrical systems. Whenever there's a power outage or damaged electrical line, these technicians are there to help. Line workers often climb to great heights, putting themselves at risk of nasty falls. They are also at risk of being electrocuted by power lines or hit by cars while working in areas with traffic.

What It Takes

- ☑ Steady hands
- ☑ Being comfortable in tight spaces
- ☑ Being unafraid of heights
- ☑ A knowledge of electrical systems
- ☑ A love of science and math

These workers wear protective equipment to stay safe from electrical sparks.

To prevent them from falling, line workers wear safety harnesses that connect them to power line poles.

Each year, thousands of line workers travel around the world to help fix power lines destroyed by hurricanes.

OUTDOOR CHAOS

Farmer

Life on the farm isn't easy . . . or safe. During hot summers and cold winters, farmers do **strenuous** work for long hours. This exposes them to weather-related dangers, including heatstroke, hypothermia, and frostbite. Farmers are also at risk from accidents caused by tractor **rollovers**. If they drive too fast or lose control of their vehicles, it can result in injuries or even death.

What It Takes

- ☑ A love for the outdoors
- ☑ Lots of stamina
- ☑ Experience with farming tools
- ☑ Strength for manual labor
- ☑ A knowledge of plants and animals
- ☑ Keen hearing

Some crops need to be handpicked by farmers, which takes a lot of hard work and strength.

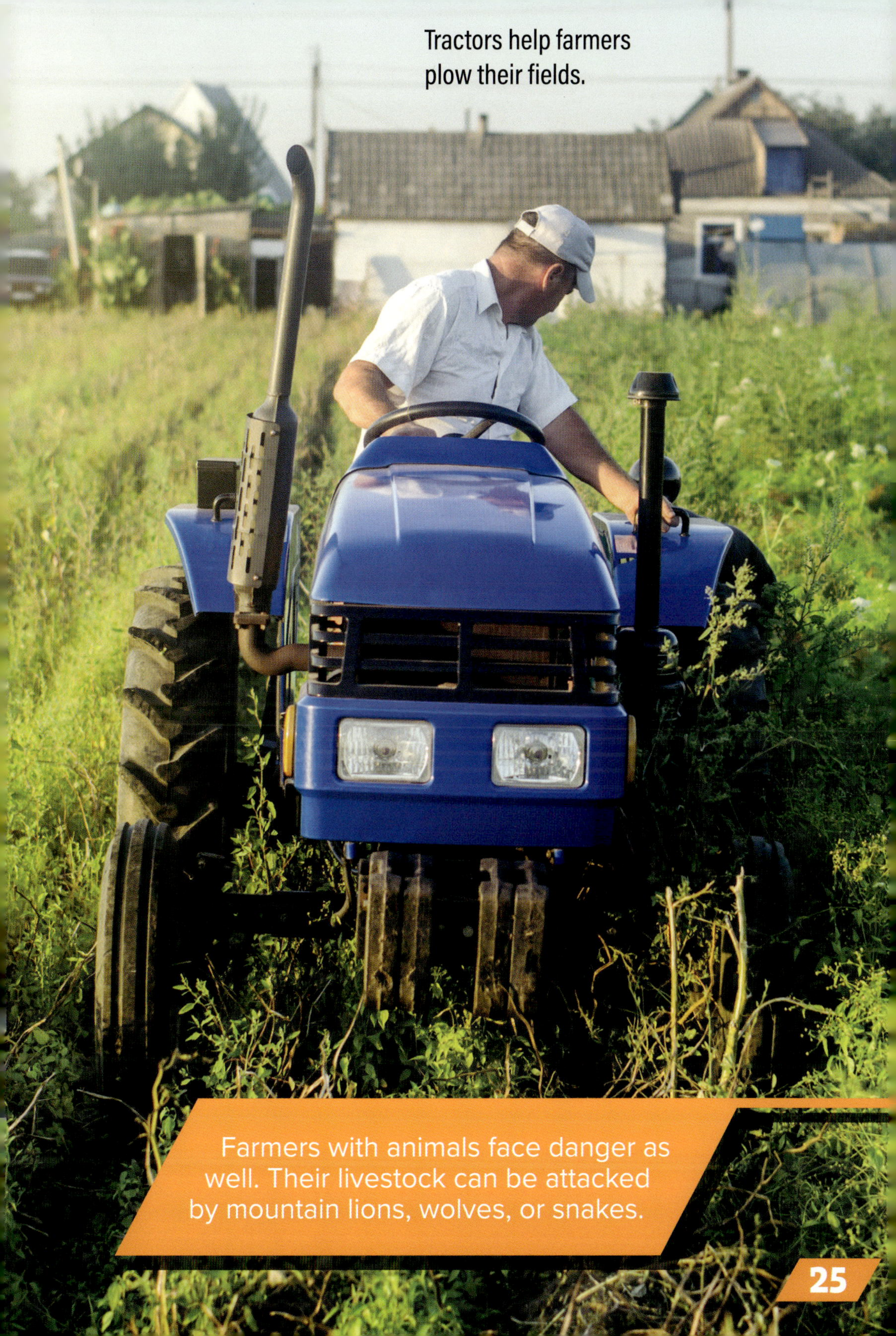

Tractors help farmers plow their fields.

Farmers with animals face danger as well. Their livestock can be attacked by mountain lions, wolves, or snakes.

HUMAN TRAFFIC LIGHTS

Crossing Guard

Not all roads have traffic lights. That's where crossing guards come in! They help **pedestrians** safely cross streets. These workers use colorful flags, whistles, or hand signals to tell traffic when to stop. Then, they allow walkers to cross. Crossing guards often wear brightly colored vests to make it easier for traffic to spot them. However, they still face the danger of getting hit by careless drivers.

What It Takes

- ☑ An ability to stand for many hours
- ☑ Communication skills
- ☑ Good judgment
- ☑ A love of rules and safety

These guards often hold signs to safely direct drivers.

Many crossing guards work at schools.

Crossing guards need to always be careful. Most pedestrian deaths are caused by traffic accidents.

LEAVE IT TO THE PROFESSIONALS

While these careers may be exciting, they also come with plenty of risks. People who rise to the challenge of dangerous careers often find their work difficult yet fulfilling. Some of these hard workers help make our lives easier and safer. Others provide us with entertainment. Whatever the case, be sure to thank them!

DANGEROUS CAREER SPOTLIGHT

Leah Penniman

Leah Penniman is a farmer. Since 2002, she's been providing people of color with tips and tricks on how to farm. But her work doesn't end on the field. Leah has published two books about farming. She also **distributes** healthy food to people who need it.

GLOSSARY

blind spots areas around vehicles that drivers are unable to see

buoy an object that floats in water to mark a spot

commercial planes airplanes used for carrying goods or people on a set schedule

distributes gives out portions of something

enforcement making sure people follow laws or rules

evidence facts or materials that help prove that a crime has taken place

hazardous very dangerous

parkour the sport of quickly moving through obstacles by climbing, jumping, and running

pedestrians people who are walking

precipitation moisture that falls from the sky, such as rain, sleet, hail, or snow

power line a cable carrying electrical power, especially one supported by pylons or poles

rigged prepared or fitted in a specific way

rollovers the overturning of vehicles

sawdust powdery particles of wood produced by sawing

scale to climb something steep, such as a wall

strenuous needing lots of energy or stamina

suspended held in place or hanging in the air

wildfires fires that spread quickly over a large area in the wilderness

READ MORE

Cella, Clara. *Smoke Jumpers (Updog Books, Dangerous Jobs).* Minneapolis: Lerner Publications, 2023.

Rhatigan, Joe. *What Farmers Need to Know (Career Expert Files).* Ann Arbor, MI: Cherry Lake Publishing, 2024.

Sommer, Nathan. *Creepy Careers (Jobs on the Edge).* Minneapolis: Bearport Publishing, 2025.

LEARN MORE ONLINE

1. Go to **FactSurfer.com** or scan the QR code below.
2. Enter "**Dangerous Careers**" into the search box.
3. Click on the cover of this book to see a list of websites.

INDEX

ABOUT THE AUTHOR

J. G. Minyard is an author who lives with his two cats in Minneapolis. He enjoys reading, writing, basketball, and playing video games.